Francis Frith's
Heart of Lancashire

Photographic Memories

Francis Frith's
Heart of Lancashire

Cliff Hayes

FRITH
BOOK Co

First published in the United Kingdom in 2001 by
Frith Book Company Ltd

Paperback Edition 2001
ISBN 1-85937-197-3

Hardback Edition 2001
1-85937-288-0

British Library Cataloguing in Publication Data

Francis Frith's Heart of Lancashire
Cliff Hayes

Frith Book Company Ltd
Frith's Barn, Teffont,
Salisbury, Wiltshire SP3 5QP
Tel: +44 (0) 1722 716 376
Email: info@frithbook.co.uk
www.frithbook.co.uk

Printed and bound in Great Britain

Front Cover: Clitheroe, from Castle Street 1921 71131

AS WITH ANY HISTORICAL DATABASE THE FRITH ARCHIVE IS CONSTANTLY BEING CORRECTED AND IMPROVED
AND THE PUBLISHERS WOULD WELCOME INFORMATION ON OMISSIONS OR INACCURACIES

Contents

Francis Frith: *Victorian Pioneer*

FRANCIS FRITH, Victorian founder of the world-famous photographic archive, was a complex and multi-talented man. A devout Quaker and a highly successful Victorian businessman, he was both philosophic by nature and pioneering in outlook.

By 1855 Francis Frith had already established a wholesale grocery business in Liverpool, and sold it for the astonishing sum of £200,000, which is the equivalent today of over £15,000,000. Now a multi-millionaire, he was able to indulge his passion for travel. As a child he had pored over travel books written by early explorers, and his fancy and imagination had been stirred by family holidays to the sublime mountain regions of Wales and Scotland. 'What a land of spirit-stirring and enriching scenes and places!' he had written. He was to return to these scenes of grandeur in later years to 'recapture the thousands of vivid and tender memories', but with a different purpose. Now in his thirties, and captivated by the new science of photography, Frith set out on a series of pioneering journeys to the Nile regions that occupied him from 1856 until 1860.

Intrigue and Adventure

He took with him on his travels a specially-designed wicker carriage that acted as both dark-room and sleeping chamber. These far-flung journeys were packed with intrigue and adventure. In his life story, written when he was sixty-three, Frith tells of being held captive by bandits, and of fighting 'an awful midnight battle to the very point of surrender with a deadly pack of hungry, wild dogs'. Sporting flowing Arab costume, Frith arrived at Akaba by camel seventy years before Lawrence, where he encountered 'desert princes and rival sheikhs, blazing with jewel-hilted swords'.

During these extraordinary adventures he was assiduously exploring the desert regions bordering the Nile and patiently recording the antiquities and peoples with his camera. He was the first photographer to venture beyond the sixth cataract. Africa was still the mysterious 'Dark Continent', and Stanley and Livingstone's historic meeting was a decade into the future. The conditions for picture taking confound belief. He laboured for hours in his wicker dark-room in the sweltering heat of the desert, while the volatile chemicals fizzed dangerously in their trays. Often he was forced to work in remote tombs and caves where conditions were cooler. Back in London he exhibited his photographs and was 'rapturously cheered' by members of the Royal Society. His reputation as a photographer was made overnight. An eminent modern historian has likened their impact on the population of the time to that on our own generation of the first photographs taken on the surface of the moon.

Venture of a Life-Time

Characteristically, Frith quickly spotted the opportunity to create a new business as a specialist publisher of photographs. He lived in an era of immense and sometimes violent change. For the poor in the early part of Victoria's reign work was a drudge and the hours long, and people had precious little free time to enjoy themselves. Most had no transport other than a cart or gig at their disposal, and had not travelled far beyond the boundaries of their own town or village. However,

by the 1870s, the railways had threaded their way across the country, and Bank Holidays and half-day Saturdays had been made obligatory by Act of Parliament. All of a sudden the ordinary working man and his family were able to enjoy days out and see a little more of the world.

With characteristic business acumen, Francis Frith foresaw that these new tourists would enjoy having souvenirs to commemorate their days out. In 1860 he married Mary Ann Rosling and set out with the intention of photographing every city, town and village in Britain. For the next thirty years he travelled the country by train and by pony and trap, producing fine photographs of seaside resorts and beauty spots that were keenly bought by millions of Victorians. These prints were painstakingly pasted into family albums and pored over during the dark nights of winter, rekindling precious memories of summer excursions.

The Rise of Frith & Co

Frith's studio was soon supplying retail shops all over the country. To meet the demand he gathered about him a small team of photographers, and published the work of independent artist-photographers of the calibre of Roger Fenton and Francis Bedford. In order to gain some understanding of the scale of Frith's business one only has to look at the catalogue issued by Frith & Co in 1886: it runs to some 670 pages, listing not only many thousands of views of the British Isles but also many photographs of most European countries, and China, Japan, the USA and Canada — note the sample page shown above from the hand-written *Frith & Co* ledgers detailing pictures taken. By 1890 Frith had created the greatest specialist photographic publishing company in the world,

with over 2,000 outlets – more than the combined number that Boots and WH Smith have today! The picture on the right shows the *Frith & Co* display board at Ingleton in the Yorkshire Dales. Beautifully constructed with mahogany frame and gilt inserts, it could display up to a dozen local scenes.

Postcard Bonanza

The ever-popular holiday postcard we know today took many years to develop. In 1870 the Post Office issued the first plain cards, with a pre-printed stamp on one face. In 1894 they allowed other publishers' cards to be sent through the mail with an attached adhesive halfpenny stamp. Demand grew rapidly, and in 1895 a new size of postcard was permitted called the court card, but there was little room for illustration. In 1899, a year after

Frith's death, a new card measuring 5.5 x 3.5 inches became the standard format, but it was not until 1902 that the divided back came into being, with address and message on one face and a full-size illustration on the other. *Frith & Co* were in the vanguard of postcard development, and Frith's sons Eustace and Cyril continued their father's monumental task, expanding the number of views offered to the public and recording more and more places in Britain, as the coasts and countryside were opened up to mass travel.

Francis Frith died in 1898 at his villa in Cannes, his great project still growing. The archive he created continued in business for another seventy years. By 1970 it contained over a third of a million pictures of 7,000 cities, towns and villages. The massive photographic record Frith has left to us stands as a living monument to a special and very remarkable man.

Frith's Archive: *A Unique Legacy*

FRANCIS FRITH'S legacy to us today is of immense significance and value, for the magnificent archive of evocative photographs he created provides a unique record of change in 7,000 cities, towns and villages throughout Britain over a century and more. Frith and his fellow studio photographers revisited locations many times down the years to update their views, compiling for us an enthralling and colourful pageant of British life and character.

We tend to think of Frith's sepia views of Britain as nostalgic, for most of us use them to conjure up memories of places in our own lives with which we have family associations. It often makes us forget that to Francis Frith they were records of daily life as it was actually being lived in the cities, towns and villages of his day. The Victorian age was one of great and often bewildering change for ordinary people, and though the pictures evoke an impression of slower times, life was as busy and hectic as it is today.

We are fortunate that Frith was a photographer of the people, dedicated to recording the minutiae of everyday life. For it is this sheer wealth of visual data, the painstaking chronicle of changes in dress, transport, street layouts, buildings, housing, engineering and landscape that captivates us so much today. His remarkable images offer us a powerful link with the past and with the lives of our ancestors.

Today's Technology

Computers have now made it possible for Frith's many thousands of images to be accessed almost instantly. In the Frith archive today, each photograph is carefully 'digitised' then stored on a CD Rom. Frith archivists can locate a single photograph amongst thousands within seconds. Views can be catalogued and sorted under a variety of categories of place and content to the immediate benefit of researchers.

Inexpensive reference prints can be created for them at the touch of a mouse button, and a wide range of books and other printed materials assembled and published for a wider, more general readership - in the next twelve months over a hundred Frith local history titles will be published! The day-to-day workings of the archive are very different from how they were in Francis Frith's time: imagine the herculean task of sorting through eleven tons of glass negatives as Frith had to do to locate a particular sequence of pictures! Yet

See Frith at www. frithbook.co.uk

the archive still prides itself on maintaining the same high standards of excellence laid down by Francis Frith, including the painstaking cataloguing and indexing of every view.

It is curious to reflect on how the internet now allows researchers in America and elsewhere greater instant access to the archive than Frith himself ever enjoyed. Many thousands of individual views can be called up on screen within seconds on one of the Frith internet sites, enabling people living continents away to revisit the streets of their ancestral home town, or view places in Britain where they have enjoyed holidays. Many overseas researchers welcome the chance to view special theme selections, such as transport, sports, costume and ancient monuments.

We are certain that Francis Frith would have heartily approved of these modern developments in imaging techniques, for he himself was always working at the very limits of Victorian photographic technology.

The Value of the Archive Today

Because of the benefits brought by the computer, Frith's images are increasingly studied by social historians, by researchers into genealogy and ancestory, by architects, town planners, and by teachers and schoolchildren involved in local history projects.

In addition, the archive offers every one of us an opportunity to examine the places where we and our families have lived and worked down the years. Highly successful in Frith's own era, the archive is now, a century and more on, entering a new phase of popularity.

The Past in Tune with the Future

Historians consider the Francis Frith Collection to be of prime national importance. It is the only archive of its kind remaining in private ownership and has been valued at a million pounds. However, this figure is now rapidly increasing as digital technology enables more and more people around the world to enjoy its benefits.

Francis Frith's archive is now housed in an historic timber barn in the beautiful village of Teffont in Wiltshire. Its founder would not recognize the archive office as it is today. In place of the many thousands of dusty boxes containing glass plate negatives and an all-pervading odour of photographic chemicals, there are now ranks of computer screens. He would be amazed to watch his images travelling round the world at unimaginable speeds through network and internet lines.

The archive's future is both bright and exciting. Francis Frith, with his unshakeable belief in making photographs available to the greatest number of people, would undoubtedly approve of what is being done today with his lifetime's work. His photographs, depicting our shared past, are now bringing pleasure and enlightenment to millions around the world a century and more after his death.

The Heart of Lancashire
An Introduction

LANCASHIRE IS A wonderful county, the very best one of all. Ask any Lancastrian: they will tell you the truth! Lancashire has many faces, and Lancastrians are so big-hearted that you would think they have more than one heart. People who think of Lancashire as consisting of just grim industrial towns have never seen the sweeping beauty of the moorlands. Those who holiday at her coastal resorts are balanced by those who get pleasure and relaxation by walking on Pendle and the other hills at the very heart of the county.

Lancashire people are like the county: they have hidden depths, and there are more sides to them than most people. A Lancashire man will fight his corner with the tenacity of a Manchester terrier, but he will soften and help you once he has won. A Lancashire lady can be full of fun, but when things go wrong she has the world's best advice and a cup of tea. Lancashire people have a wonderful dry sense of humour and an ability to laugh at themselves. While in other areas people 'take the mickey' and poke fun at each other, in Lancashire they laugh with you, not at you. Sarcastic they may be, but they are gentle with it.

This book is a collection of memories from both sides of the heart of Lancashire. Firstly we see the villages of the Ribble Valley, an area of outstanding beauty, and we follow the Ribble and Hodder from

the Yorkshire border down to Preston. Then we turn south and go into the industrial heartland. There we find the coal mining area, the very centre of Lancashire, that did so much for the war effort; and the cotton area, with its large mills.

I think we are very fortunate that the Frith team has covered this area so well in the past. They have recorded very thoroughly an area that is often seen as being off the beaten track. I was faced with over one hundred great photographs of the towns and villages in and around the Ribble Valley and the heart of Lancashire, and I wondered how to attack the problem. Alphabetically, the book would jump all over the place, so I thought that perhaps I should go from north to south - I was not sure. Then it dawned on me that every one of these villages and towns was on water. Whether it was stream, burn, water, river or even the Leeds to Liverpool canal, every town and village was next to some water. So I have laid the book out following the rivers of the area. Just as ancient man did, so this volume follows the rivers from upstream down. I hope that you agree with our choice of photographs, and that you have a pleasant journey down the streams.

Our book shows views and scenes that have not been in print for many years. I hope the book makes you visit the area to see the secrets of Lancashire. Visit the Trough of Bolland and Pendle - these are truly areas of unspoilt beauty, and are hidden gems in the very heart of Lancashire.

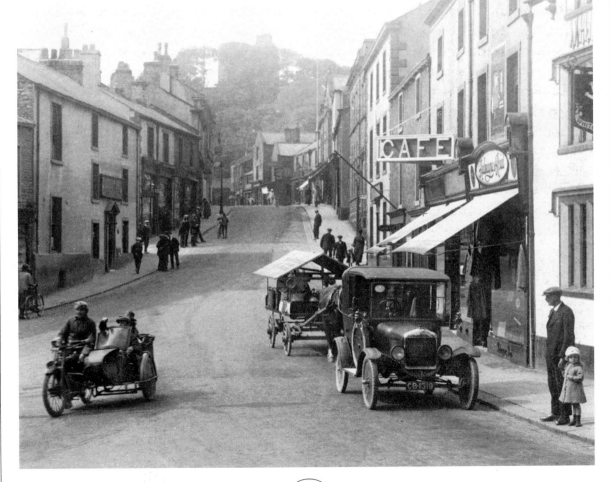

On the River Hodder:
High in the Hills

The name Hodder means 'pleasant stream'. It is a Celtic name, and it describes the river well. Rising on Lamb Hill Fell, the river now runs into the Stock Reservoir and then resumes its wandering in North Lancashire. In an area dominated by rivers, crossing them has always been a problem. The smaller rivers were crossed on planks and stepping stones. Then came fords: cutting the banks to widen rivers makes them shallow enough to drive or walk across. This worked in many places for centuries; but then the need to be able to cross in all weathers, at all times of the year, meant bridges had to be built. One of the most famous of the area's bridges, and certainly one of the oldest on the Hodder, is near Hurst Green (Stoneyhurst).

The River Hodder, The Bridges 1894 34339a
Here we see the pack-horse bridge at Hurst Green. The newer road bridge, built in 1826, is behind it. Clitheroe and Great Mitton are to the right, and Stoneyhurst to the left. In 1648 Oliver Cromwell himself led 4,000 men across that old bridge in single file. He had stayed the night at Stoneyhurst, and it took most of the day for the horses, mules and men to cross. The bridge was built in the mid 1500s at a cost of £70, and was paid for by Richard Shireburn, lord of the manor. It is still there today; it is being restored at the moment, as it was deemed unsafe by the authorities.

**Slaidburn
Church Street 1921**
71212
Now very much part of
Lancashire, the village
of Slaidburn was in
Yorkshire at the time of
our photograph. Slaid
means 'flat marshy
ground', burn is the Old
English word for brook,
so the name means 'flat
marshy ground by the
brook', which describes
the area well. The Black
Bull public house on
the left was later to
become a Youth Hostel.
Note the very large
board with the
landlord's name (A
Walker) on it. This was
the local custom at the
turn of the 19th/20th
century, and it led to
many pubs taking the
landlord's name or
nickname as their name
in later years. This is
where Church Street
meets Chapel Street.
On the right we see the
famous Hark to Bounty
Inn, which was used as
an area court house.

◀ **Slaidburn**
Hammerton Hall 1921
71217
This is the most
northerly of all the
photographs in our
book. The Hall lies in a
crook of the River
Hodder, with a stream
called Barn Gill and its
waterfall in the Hall
grounds. The bridge in
the foreground is over
the Barn Gill.
Hammerton Hall is really
an enlarged and fortified
farm-house.

◄ Slaidburn, Town End c1955
S139007

Slaidburn nestles in a hollow with higher ground around it. As well as the River Hodder at the east of the village, it has Crossdale Brook running through it. That brook has a weir just before it enters the village, which was built to keep the water deeper for a mill that was here two centuries ago. It was at Slaidburn that many of the ancient pack-horse trails used to meet or cross. Here we see the outskirts of Slaidburn.

▼ Dunsop Bridge, Brennand Valley 1921 71231

This lovely view was taken just a few miles north of Dunsop Bridge. We can see the tiny River Brennand running down to join the Whitendale River to make the River Dunsop, which gives the town its name. The Ordnance Survey department has declared Dunsop Bridge to be the village nearest to the exact centre of the British Isles.

◄ Dunsop Bridge
The Hodder Bridge 1921
71220

This splendid view of the River Hodder shows the magnificent scenery of the area. The photograph shows the scene as it could have been 100 years earlier, except for the gas pipe crossing the river in the bottom left-hand corner. Hidden among the trees in the centre of our photograph is a foot (and animal) bridge just a few miles outside Dunsop Bridge. The hill on the left is called Knot or Sugar Loaf.

◄ **Whitewell, St Michael's Church 1921** 71250
Whitewell is a really small village: this medieval
church and the Whitewell Inn are the only
buildings of any note or size. Many members of
the royal family have in the past stayed at the inn
whilst hunting, or whilst travelling round England.

▼ **Whitewell, General View 1921** 71245
When our photograph was taken, Whitewell
really was just a small and remote community.
Being so near the old Roman road from
Manchester to York, and being so well-placed on
many routes, it has always had a reputation for
putting up visitors and travellers. There was once
a royal hunting forest next to Whitewell, and that
brought in the aristocracy of past times.

The River Ribble and above Clitheroe

The River Ribble is one of the major rivers in the north-west of England. It rises on the border with Yorkshire, and tumbles down the hillsides to meet up with the River Hodder and the River Calder to gather strength before pushing on to Preston and the coast. This area where the three rivers meet is one that has sustained life since man arrived in the area. The fact that there are so many streams and burns feeding into the river system makes the area even more fascinating. Every village has a river or a stream; the water was so pure that it was the drinking water, the ale and the washing machine of the community. Some of the villages have been forced to change their allegiances over the years, for the Lancashire and Yorkshire border has been moved more than once. Here we look at the villages on and around the upper reaches of the River Ribble.

Gisburn, The Village 1921 71203
The road running through the village is the A59 from Clitheroe to Skipton. Note the New Inn on the left of the picture, and how large the name-board of the publican was. The village policeman in his cape stands in the middle of the road. Guy of Gisburn, of Robin Hood fame, was said to have come from this village. In 1260 a charter was granted to the Abbot of Sawley Abbey to hold a fair in Gisburn. The width of the street shows that the village was laid out with room for the country market that was once held here, with stalls on the cobbles either side. Some of the cottages go back to the 1500s. The local lords were the Lister family, many of whom lie in the small village church.

Gisburn, The Village 1921 71202
The name of the village had an 'e' on the end until the railway company put up their sign spelt 'Gisburn', and the 'e' was forgotten. Mentioned in the Domesday Book, the village has always been a magnet for visitors and day-trippers. Here we see the main street, and two cars parked outside the Ribblesdale Arms. Once a year the village would be packed with visitors; they came to lean over Paythorne Bridge and watch the salmon leaping in the River Ribble. Salmon Sunday was still popular into the 1960s, and it is making a revival today. One of the Lister family built Gisburn Hall and Gisburn Park. Now a hospital, it was later the home of the Ribblesdale family. I wonder what the bunting is celebrating?

Bolton by Bowland
The Church Gates 1921 71208
This is a charming photograph of the area outside the churchyard
entrance. Many refer to this village as the most perfect in Lancashire;
with its village green next to the church, and an old inn across the
road, it is just how we all imagine an old English village ought to look.
In the church is the famous Pudsay Chapel: the large local marble lid
of Sir Ralph Pudsay's tomb has carvings of himself and his three wives
and his twenty-five children. It is large, 3 metres by 2 metres, to fit
them all in. The church is dedicated to St Peter and St Paul. Its history
is unique, for a king helped in its design. Henry VI is said to have lived
here in Bolton Hall for a year or so while hiding from the Yorkists in
1464 after losing the Battle of Hexham. King Henry's Well is near the
village: it is said to have been found and dug by Henry. The villagers
put up a bathhouse over the spring which is still there today.

▼ **Bolton by Bowland, The Green 1921** 71206

We see the Green from the far side. The village (the name means 'the dwelling by the bow of the river') has two greens; because it was all part of the Pudsay estate, there was no pressure to expand or to pull down and rebuild. The right-hand side of the building at the end of the path was at one time the old Court House. You can tell it by the larger first-floor windows: they let in more light for the Lord of the Manor and the visiting judges, as they sat and listened to cases concerning the Forrest and Trough law.

▼ **Barnoldswick, Tubber Hill c1920** B589004

Barnoldswick is pronounced 'Barlick' by the locals. This is another village that has moved with boundary changes. It has been in Yorkshire longer than in Lancashire, but Lancashire is where it is now - so we can include it. Do not shout too loud about it, though, as there are many locals who would rather it were back across the border. Tubber Hill is on the outskirts of Barnoldswick; running alongside it is part of the Roman road which once went from Preston to York.

▲ **Barnoldswick, Church Street 1952** B589011
Church Street leads down to St. Mary-le-Gill church. It was built around 1160 on the edge of the town by Cistercian monks, who found the natives not very friendly when they tried to establish an abbey here in 1147. The Commercial Hotel can be seen on the left, with two local men passing the time of day. Savage's and Burton's Menswear shop are on the right, and there is a cafe further up the street.

◀ **Barnoldswick, The Locks c1955** B589007
Barnoldswick grew once the Leeds-Liverpool canal arrived around 1812. The local textile industry blossomed, and people moved into the village from the surrounding areas to work in the new mills. Quarries sprang up, and jobs were created. Here we see a section of the canal at Greenberfield Locks, just before it enters the town. This is the highest point that the canal reaches. The revival in pleasure boats on the canals has brought back a lot of life to the area.

Grindleton
The Village 1921 71175

Grindleton is a classic case of village development: here ancient roads cross, and ribbon building took place along those roads. Many of the old houses were weaver's cottages, built in a time when hand-loom weaving was the major industry in the area. The road from Sawley to Waddington crossed the back road from Clitheroe to Slaidburn here, so the cloth produced from local wool could be taken to the markets and fairs on packhorses. We are looking up from the bottom of the village. 'H Smalley, Grocer & General Dealer, licensed to sell tobacco and cigars', says the sign on the left. The assistant peeps out of the shop, and there are two other ladies sitting in the first floor window, keeping an eye on the goings-on.

Grindleton
The Village and the Post Office 1921 71173
The post office is on the left with its sign outside.
At the time of this photograph, the population of
the village had almost halved: local cottage
industries had declined, and the arrival of the new
mills in the larger towns meant that people flocked
there to live and work.

**Chatburn
The Village 1921**
71178
Here we see motorists in the village - they are probably touring the area. The 'burn' part of the name comes from the stream which runs through the village. The 'chat' part is either an Old English personal name 'Ceatta', or the word 'ceat', which means 'piece of wet ground'. In our view we are looking towards the bridge over the burn. The Brown Cow public house is on the right, and the Black Bull Hotel can just be made out further down the road. The village is 400ft above sea level.

Chatburn
The Village 1921
71177
We are at the top of the street seen in photograph No 71178. The Black Bull, where the people are standing, was built in 1855; it was a Blackburn Brewery Company pub, and so was the Brown Cow. Can you see the two motor bikes and sidecars in our photograph? These were very popular in the inter-war years with young people, for they were a cheap form of transport. The one nearest the camera seems to have the lady driving and the gentleman in the sidecar.

▼ **West Bradford, The Village 1921** 71150

West Bradford gets its name from being west of the broad, shallow ford of the River Ribble. Again, we see a large painted board; this one proclaims that James Leeming was proprietor of the Three Millstones Inn on the right of our photograph. Eaves Hall, next to the village, is now a country club for the Civil Service Motoring Association. The cottages on the left were a Mission Room before the church of St Catherine was built in 1898.

▼ **Waddington, The Village 1899** 42914

In this picture we can see the small stream that runs down from Waddington Fell and the Moorcock Inn as it runs right through the centre of the village to join the Ribble. It was at Waddington Old Hall that Henry VI took refuge after leaving Bolton-by-Bowland, and it was here that he was betrayed and captured in nearby Clitheroe Wood. The church of St Helen, with its 15th-century tower, can be seen on the skyline. It was largely rebuilt, but in keeping with the original style, in 1901. Many of the Parker family from nearby Browsholme Hall are buried here in the church, and they have their own chapel and pews.

▲ **Waddington**
The Almshouses 1899
42916

The apron, or uniform, on the lady in our photograph reminds us that these almshouses were also referred to as Waddington Hospital. The child on the donkey next to her could have been recuperating. In 1706 Robert Parker paid for the building of these almshouses to accommodate twenty-nine widows and spinsters of the parish. They were moved to this site around the village green just over a century later.

◀ **Waddington, Coronation Bridge c1960** W523007
In an area of outstanding beauty and ancient and quaint villages, its hard to be noticed. But the village of Waddington has won the 'Best Kept Village in Lancashire' title on many occasions for being just that little bit more beautiful. When Queen Elizabeth II came to the throne in 1953, the village erected a Coronation Bridge and laid out Coronation Gardens, which we can see here. The name Waddington means 'the settlement of Wada' (a Saxon chief). Waddow Hall stands close to the village.

Clitheroe
Bungerley Bridge 1894 34346
The River Ribble in summer is the most pleasant of rivers, and to
picnic and paddle by its banks has been a delight for many
centuries. Here we see a photograph of children enjoying a day at
Bungerley Bridge, north of Clitheroe. The young lad in the centre is
obviously proud of his boat, but the young ladies on the right do
not look too happy, do they? Waddow Hall, at the north side of the
bridge, is a 16th-century building with additions of 1630. It was the
home of the dowager lady of the Tempest family; it was bought by
the Girl Guide Association in 1928.

The Castle Town of Clitheroe

'A township, parochial chapelry, market town, corporate and parliamentary borough', was how Clitheroe was described in 1840. The Honour of Clitheroe, held in medieval times by the de Lacy family, comprised the parishes of Blackburn, Chipping, Ribchester, Bury, Rochdale and the Forest of Bowland; its 28,800 acres were all controlled and run from the Castle. The Charter of Incorporation for Clitheroe was granted in 1147, making it the second oldest town in Lancashire. Clitheroe has many folk tales and curious legends associated with it and the surrounding region. Peg o' the Well and the

Leper's Inheritance are two good examples - I wish there was space here to re-tell these stories. Another fascinating tale is that of James King, born in Clitheroe, the son of the local vicar, who sailed as 2nd Lieutenant on Captain Cook's ship the 'Resolution'. When there was a major overhaul of the council system in 1974, Clitheroe was the natural headquarters for the newly-formed Ribble Valley Authority. Clitheroe 'is half in Lancashire and half in fairyland': this lovely description is by the historian H V Morton, and depicts the loveliness of the countryside around here very well.

Clitheroe, From the Castle 1921 71129
We are looking down from the keep of Clitheroe Castle to the town below. Castle Street is in the foreground; it changes to Church Street at the Library (the triangular building with the clock), which was built in 1905. Church Street leads to the large parish church of St Mary Magdalene; its 15th-century tower is topped by a twisted spire, which was added in 1846. The Swan & Royal Hotel stands out on the right of the street, one of the many eating and drinking places on Castle Street.

Clitheroe
Castle Street 1921
71133
Castle Street is
Clitheroe's main
shopping street. Shops
here have been kept by
the same families for
years, and they still
have a reputation for
quality and service. A
wine merchant's shop
run for over a century
by the same family, a
butcher making
sausages using recipes
his great-grandfather
used 80 years ago -
these are in King and
Castle Streets. In this
photograph the shops
look quite busy.
Tuesday and Saturday
are market days, and
the town is packed with
villagers coming in from
miles around.
Wednesday is still half-
day closing. We can see
how the Castle
dominates the street,
even though only its
keep is still standing.
The Starkie Arms Hotel
is on the far right of our
photograph. Notice the
stage-coach arch next
to the bay windows: the
stage coaches to
Preston and Blackburn
left from here.

**Clitheroe
From Castle Street
1921** 71131
Our photographer
stood in Church Street;
the part we see is
Market Place, where the
early markets took
place. The White Lion
Hotel on the right is still
there today, and so is
W D Cunliffe the
grocers and bakers
(telephone 123). Next
to them, out of the
picture, is now the
Clitheroe Information
Centre. Three doors
down on the right, with
a horse-drawn
vegetable cart in front,
is the Victoria Hotel, on
the corner of King
Street. I have enjoyed
many a Sunday lunch
there. All four of the
hotels on Castle Street
do very good meals.
The cafe next door had
Taylor & Hughes as
proprietors in 1921:
their slogan was 'we are
noted for our pork pies'.

Clitheroe
Castle Street 1921
71130
We are outside the
Swan & Royal. The sign
seems to say it all: a
garage is provided for
the modern motor car,
bait for those who
come for the fishing,
and stables for the
horses. The hotel was
originally the Swan; it
was visited by the travel
writer John Byng, who
in 1792 reported that
his bedroom door was
broken and everyone
could see him in bed.
Apart from the castle,
this is the highest part
of Clitheroe, 300ft
above sea level. It is
here that the morris and
folk dancing takes place
once a year at the
Clitheroe Folk Festival,
an event not to be
missed. The second
shop on the left of our
picture is the offices of
the local newspaper,
the 'Advertiser & Times'.
In 1921 they also had a
lending library, with
maps for motorists and
a fountain pen repair
department.

Clitheroe, The Castle 1927 80535

The Inner Keep is on the right, with holes knocked into its 9ft-thick walls. It is the smallest Norman keep in England, and last saw action at the end of the Civil War, when Colonel Ashton's forces barricaded themselves in the castle demanding the pay that was owed them. Parliament had the castle and its chapel dismantled, so that no-one could ever defy the Commonwealth again. The buildings on the left date from c1725, when the Crown owned the castle; it is now a museum of Ribble life. The North-West Sound Archives are also based here, which do marvellous work recording people talking of their lives. Roger de Pictou was granted the land between the Mersey and the Ribble, but he soon fell out of favour; Ilbert de Lacy built the castle - he was given the land from here to Pontefract. The last of the family was hung for treason to the Crown. It has been the property of the Duke of Albermarle, the Duke of Buccleuch and Lord Montagu of Beaulieu. This last family formed the Clitheroe Castle Estate Ltd in order to sell the castle and all the feudal rights which went with it to the people of Clitheroe. In 1919, amid the pain and sadness after the First World War, the people of Clitheroe raised £15,000 to buy the Castle and its grounds, and a Garden of Remembrance was laid out. The statue of the soldier with his rifle upside-down was put up shortly afterwards.

Clitheroe, From the Castle 1927 80530

We are looking north towards Kemple End. The first sod of the railway line at Clitheroe was cut on 30 December 1846. The large railway sidings that we can see here denote how important Clitheroe was as a distribution centre for this part of the Ribble Valley. After the livestock market on Monday (the sheep market), Tuesday and Friday, animals would head out all over Lancashire. The origin of the name Clitheroe is surrounded by doubts and mystery. The 'oe' at the end comes from the Old English 'hoh', meaning a hill or promontory. The 'Clith' part could come from OE 'clyde', stones or rocky. (The name had a 'd' in it until around 1650; the spellings 'Cliderhou', 'Clyderhowe' also appear in the past). 'The hill of lime or loose stones' is one meaning suggested in a recent book, or if we believe the name has a Celtic derivation, we end up with 'the shelter on a rock'; but no one can really pin the meaning down. One of Clitheroe's famous sons is Jimmy Clitheroe, who made us all laugh in the early days of radio - he really did come from Clitheroe. A family member keeps a cafe, Jimmy Clitheroe's, next to the market in the town centre; it has photographs and memorabilia all over the walls.

Around the Hill named Pendle

Pendle is a hill. To be a mountain you have to be over 2,000ft above sea level. Though parts of Pendle Hill reach over 1,900ft, it never quite makes it to the mountain mark. The name means hill: 'Pen' comes from the Celtic word for hill, and the 'dle' was added later to denote a hill (pen-hyll). It is a very dominant feature of the landscape, and yet locals tell me it feels as if it protects them, rather than looms over them. Because of the famous Pendle witch trials in 1612, the hill has gained a reputation for sorcery and evil deeds. Those who know the area treat these superstitious tales with a pinch of salt, but they do not deny that the quick changes in weather, which bring down the clouds over the hill, certainly add to the brooding mystery of Pendle Hill. The beauty of the place inspired George Fox, the founder of the Quaker movement, when he was here in the mid 15th century, and many poets have written about this lovely area.

Worston, The Village 1921 71160
Worston once stood astride the main A59 road, but now it is happy to be a quiet backwater in the shadow of Pendle. This sleepy scene is typical of the lovely villages in the area.

Downham
The Village 1894

34357

Children pose near the small bridge over Downham Beck, a brook which runs through the heart of the village. Downham is another example of a village which was tightly controlled by the lords of the manor, who refused to let industry into the village. The Dinelay family were first, then the Asshetons took over the village in 1588. In 1953 the head of the Assheton family was created Lord Clitheroe, and the family are still taking care of the village today. They have twice rebuilt St Leonard's church, which we can see on the left in the background. Parts of the church date from the 1400s, and the three bells are said to have come from the Abbey after it was pulled down.

Downham, The Village 1895 35716

The name Downham means 'dwelling by the hill' - the hill is obviously Pendle, which can be seen in the background. This photograph is unfortunate in that it makes the village look a little ramshackle, but in truth it was anything but. The Asshetons looked after their village, and made sure everything was in order. Everyone in the village had a job on the estate, and everyone had a place in the village society. The Roman road from Ribchester to Ikley passes through Downham Park at the end of the village. The grave of Roman soldiers killed in a skirmish with the Brigantes is said to be marked with a large stone to the left of the gates to the Hall.

Downham, The Village 1921 71189

This rather posed picture shows the lower part of the village. The two men, one holding the horse and one with his dog, are everything a photographer could want in a village scene. The two ladies sitting on the grass add charm to the picture, which is typical of Downham, a well-managed, working, but historical place. You can see the 15th-century tower of the village church peeping out on the skyline on the left. The church has some very fierce-looking gargoyles; it is the last resting-place of many of the Assheton family, who have their own chapel and vault there.

Downham, The Post Office and the Old Stocks 1921 71190
Our photographer was a busy man, and obviously spent a week or more travelling
the area to capture the village scenes that we see here in our book, some eighty
years on. One of his briefs was to include the local Post Office in his photographs, so
that it could then be turned into a postcard to sell in the shop. Here we see the Post
Office complete with children and a horse and trap outside. On the right an old
sycamore tree shades what is left of the village stocks. The film 'Whistle Down The
Wind' with Hayley Mills was filmed in and around Downham village.

Hurst Green
The Cross c1950 H445011

This is the T-junction at the centre of Hurst Green, seen here in the gentle post-war years. This stretch of road has a history all of its own. In 1826 J C Macadam laid a new road surface here as a trial. Hundreds of locals came to see it, and 'tarmacadam' became a huge success. This is the Shirburne's village; it was started by the family to house estate workers, and servants from nearby Stonyhurst, whose entrance is on the left. 'Refreshments', 'Teas', 'Hovis' - these are all signs that show us that this was a tourist spot. The Eagle & Child Inn reflects a marriage with the Stanley family, and the Shirburne Arms (formerly the Three Fishes) is just off camera on the right. Three fishes was on the badge of the Abbot of Whalley in times past, and the sign pops up all over the area.

Stonyhurst College 1899 43489
There are two of these large
man-made ponds at the front of
the college. This, the left-hand
one, is always full of ducks and
other wild fowl. The house, which
was at one time the largest
building in the north of England,
was built by Sir Nicolas Sherburn
(Shirburn) around 1690. His son
and heir died in 1702 aged 9
from eating yew berries, and the
family died out. The estate was
left to a cousin (named Weld)
who gave it to the Jesuits in 1794
- they needed a new home after
being thrown out of Belgium. The
estate is over 2,000 acres, much
of which is farmed. The church
of St Peter can be seen to the
right of the picture. The college is
open to visitors during the
summer holidays, and is well
worth visiting. It has a library that
contains mementoes of many
famous people, including Bonnie
Prince Charlie and Mary Queen
of Scots.

**Little Mitton
The Hall 1894** 34344
Today, Little Mitton Hall
is an hotel. Mitton means
'the village where the
streams meet'. The
Hodder and the Ribble
meet here, and that is
what gave the area its
name. Great Mitton is on
the north bank of the
river, and Little, or Lower
Mitton on the south
bank, with the River
Ribble (which we can see
here) in between.

Whalley, Accrington Road 1901 47063
The T-junction and the church are just ahead. Whalley had an abbey once, and that fact distracts from the importance of the church here. The church of St Mary and All Saints has ancient crosses in the churchyard and a thousand years of history. In the grounds it has a sundial from the 1700s. The biggest problem for visitors to Whalley today is where to park. The abbey and its grounds have passed through many hands since being seized by Henry VIII, but it is now back in the hands of the church. Much of the pulled-down abbey found its way into the church, including the misericords.

▼ **Whalley, Broad Lane 1906** 54210

Here we have a grand view of the railway arches heading out of Whalley. The railway arrived in the village in 1850, and the 600yd-long viaduct carries the Blackburn to Clitheroe line through at a height of 70ft. This means that double-decker buses and coaches cannot head north out of Whalley towards Mitton. Whalley is just a village, though a large one; it is always high on the best-kept village awards list, a title which it has won in the past. The last Abbot of Whalley, a Cistercian monk, is thought to be buried in the parish church after being hung for opposing Henry VIII.

▼ **Whalley, King Street 1921** 71116

Whalley means 'the clearing or field by the hill', and we can see how close the hill, known as Whalley Cob, is from our photograph. Here we see the main street, with a policeman on traffic duty at the junction with Accrington Road outside the Whalley Arms. The River Calder runs through the village; it was here that a mass baptism took place when Christianity first arrived in around 626-7 AD. The church here was once the mother church for half of Lancashire (47 townships and three large villages). One of Whalley's famous sons was Samuel Brooks, who moved to Manchester to make his fortune - he named an area that he purchased there Whalley Range. On King Street and the corner of Station Road is an old cricket square. This is said to be where the first Lancashire versus Yorkshire match was played.

▲ **Sabden, The Wesleyan Church and Wesley Street c1960** S691011

This photograph was taken fro Wesley Street. It was only a m away that George Fox, the Quaker, stood on the 'nick' of Pendle in 1652 and declared himself moved to start a religious order, the Society of Friends. Sabden is unique in t it was almost an industrial villa It had six mills at one time, an yet it sits astride the old pack-horse trails in a green and remote area within Pendle's rir It will always be connected wit Richard Cobden, the reformer who owned one of the mills here - much of his wealth cam from that mill. Sabden was no for its production of gentleme handkerchiefs for a time. Sabden's 'Treacle Mine' was a well, or spring, whose water w used to 'treat all' complaints.

◄ Pendleton
The Village 1921 71164
Pendleton nestles right in the shadow of Pendle Hill: in fact, the name means 'the houses on Pendle'. Owned for centuries by the Aspinall family, Pendleton was an old village when the Domesday Book was compiled. With its stream running down the middle of the village, Pendleton seems to present an idyllic picture.

Pendleton, The Village 1921 71165

The houses are built of local stone. The stream meanders through the centre of the village, and local children play pooh sticks and just watch the stream. The fortunes of the village have fluctated with time, and week-enders and in-comers now make up a large part of the old village. The village was once nicknamed 'the goose village', because it was said that geese from Pendleton tasted better than any others in Lancashire.

Ribchester, The Church 1894 34325

The church is dedicated to St.Wilfrid, the Archbishop of York in the 660s. Wilfrid is a northern dedication, and usually denotes an ancient church. Ribchester was once a Roman fort (Bremetennacum), and it was situated by an important ford of the River Ribble. In front of the church is the graveyard; here it is not looking at its best, and very uneven. The fact that the churchyard is circular suggests that it follows the line of some earlier Roman structure. Nearby is Ribchester Museum, which is devoted to the Romans who lived here more than 1,500 years ago.

Colne Water and the River Calder

We move to the third of our three rivers, and go high into the hills to find Colne Water. The area used to be known as Marsden. Great Marsden covers what is now called Colne, and Little Marsden was known as Nelson down to Reedley. Walverton Water ran between the two Marsdens.

The district was entirely dependent on agriculture two hundred years ago; it slowly turned to the wool industry, then to cotton, and now it has a mixture of light and heavy industry and engineering. Coal mining was once a prosperous industry here.

A composite postcard of Colne produced by Francis Frith c1960
The top left picture reminds us of the town's connection with the famous jam-making firm, William Hartley. Hartley's used much of its money to put things back into the community, including a hospital and an elderly people's home. Another Hartley, Wallace, also from Colne, was on the 'Titanic'; he gained fame by being the leader of the orchestra that played 'Nearer My God To Thee' as the ship sank. The ruins of Wycoller Hall, with its Bronte connection, lie just north of Colne.

▼ Colne, The Church c1960 C60010

The oldest building in Colne is the church. St Bartholomew's dates from the 1200s, and much of the 62ft tower is original. The church has stocks and a charnel house in the graveyard. What an idyllic scene this is, complete with thatched houses and even a spreading chestnut tree. The name Colne means 'roaring river'.

▼ Nelson, Manchester Road c1955 N146011

The story of how the town got its name is an unusual one. When the railway arrived, a station was built here at Marsden. There was another Marsden just a few miles up the line in Yorkshire, so a railway official gave the station the name of the inn that was next to the station. The inn was called the Lord Nelson, after the famous admiral. The station's name was was shortened to Nelson to make the sign smaller, and the name stuck; the whole area has been known as Nelson ever since. The first meeting of the Local Board was held here on 17 December 1864, and the town became a borough on 21 July 1890. There are two very large churches in Nelson, and we can see them both in our photograph. St Mary's, with its very tall spire and eleven bells, has two stained glass windows executed by Burne Jones.

▲ Nelson Leeds Road c1955

N146052

The Borough Hotel is on the right of our photograph; this was a Dutton House. Woolworth's is a little further up the street, and then we see the Town Hall, with its unusual spire and clock. Built in 1881, the Town Hall was extended in 1891 and again in 1935. The Corporation once operated a light railway to Barrowford and Colne from here.

◄ **Nelson**
Town Centre c1955
N146033
We are looking down
Manchester Road, the A56;
the road looks quiet and
almost asleep. The Lord
Nelson Hotel is on the right.
This is not the original one
which gave the town its
name, but a later one built
on the same spot.

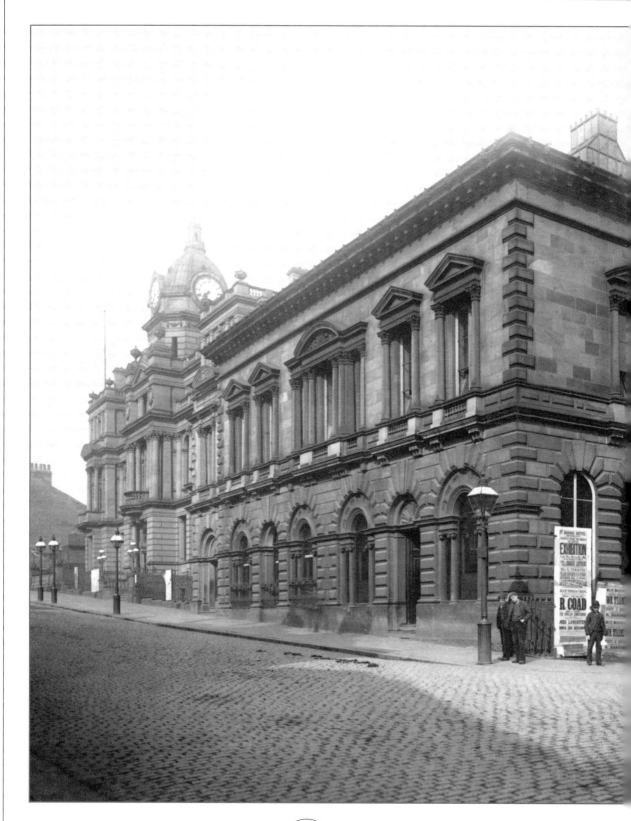

Burnley

Burnley means 'the place by the river Brun'; the town snuggles in a valley between the rivers Calder and Brun. All the early forms of the name begin 'Bru', with the 'r' before 'u': Brunlea (1230), Brunleya (1230), Brunley (1251), and Bronlelay (1305). It was 1434 before we find the 'u' in front of the 'r' and it is spelt Burnley. The Brun joins the River Calder just two miles from Burnley. A nickname for the locals is 'Burnley Mashers': 'masher' is a shortened form of 'smasher', a bit of a dandy. As with so many other towns in the area, it was the Leeds and Liverpool canal which brought about the growth of Burnley, and there is a large piece of that canal history alive and well at the Weaver's Triangle on the Burnley Wharf, Manchester Road. There were once 200 mills and industrial chimneys pouring smoke into the air of Burnley. There were also once over 80 coal mines in the area, but all have now gone; the last one, Hopton Valley, closed in 1982.

Burnley, The Mechanics' Institute 1895 35787
The Institute was opened in 1855 by Colonel Charles Townley; it was a haven for apprentices taking on night-school to further their careers, and for youngsters wanting to better themselves. It is still there today as an Arts Centre and the Tourist Information Centre. Burnley Town Hall peeps out from behind the Institute. The Institute held school prize givings as well as large dinners; then it became the New Empress Night Club in 1963, and after that a Bingo Hall. Queen Elizabeth II came and re-opened the restored, re-designed Mechanics Institute on 12 November 1987.

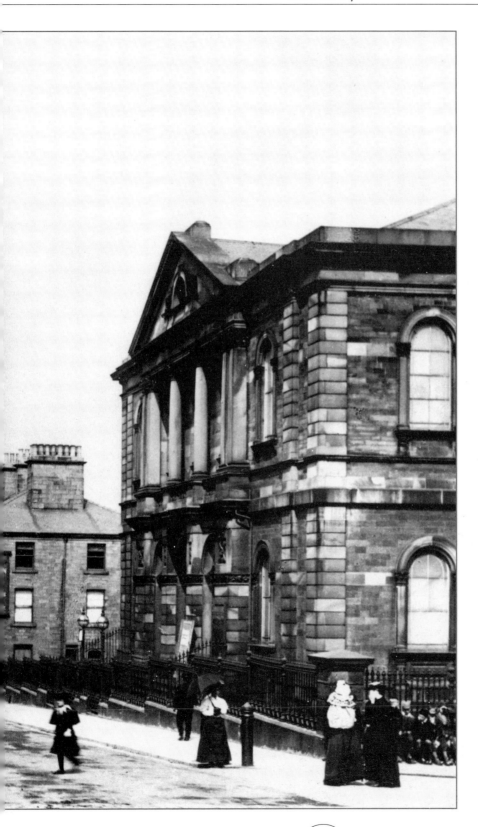

**Burnley, Manchester
Road 1895** 35789
On the right is the
United Free Methodist
Church, which opened
in 1869, and facing it
on the left is Burnley
Town Hall. The Town
Hall was built in 1888; it
was completed in the
October of that year to
a design by Holton &
Fox of Dewsbury, at a
cost of £50,000. It is
built of Yorkshire stone
in a classical
Renaissance style.

Burnley
Duke Bar 1906 54183
Duke Bar is on the
outskirts of Burnley.
The Duke of York public
house can be seen in
the centre of our
picture. Burnley was
one of the few towns
where steam trams
were employed after
the horse buses and
before the electric
trams that the
corporation introduced
in the early 1900s.
Note the wonderfully-
lettered sign for the
Duke Bar Bottle Stores
on the left of the
picture, which
promotes 'Grimshaw's
Lancastrian Ales &
Stout'. The railway
arrived in Burnley from
Accrington in
September 1848, and
six months later the line
went on to Colne. The
railway had a large
impact on the town,
especially as there was
so much coal mining in
the area.

Burnley, Scott Park 1896 37408
Scott Park was opened on 18 August 1895; it was named after Alderman Scott, who had died in 1891 leaving £10,000 in his will to open a public park. In this photograph it looks rather new and un-developed, as indeed it was at this time. Some said that Burnley did not need parks, as the Pennines of South Lancashire are only ten minutes away, and some lovely countryside surrounds the town.

Burnley, The Entrance to Townley Park 1895 35800
The castellated entrance to Townley Hall, on the A671 Todmorden Road at Burnley Wood, was photographed when it was still a private estate. The Townley family owned the hall for over 500 years; it was given to the people of Burnley by the last occupant, Lady O'Hagan, the widow of Lord O'Hagan, former Lord Chancellor of Ireland. Born Alice Mary Townley, she was a great lady. She took the family motto, 'rank has its obligations', to her heart, and was tireless in her work for the people of Burnley, especially the less fortunate. In March 1902 she sold the hall and its 62 acres to Burnley for the very low price of £17,500, and she gave some of the money back to pay for the art gallery it was to house. Townley Hall opened as a public park on 18 June 1902. Lady O'Hagan died in 1921, and the whole town of Burnley closed down on the day of her funeral. It was a mark of respect to a truly regal lady.

Burnley
Townley Hall 1906 54201

Townley Hall was first opened to the people of Burnley on 20 May 1903. The opening ceremony was performed by the Earl of Roseberry. Like many old houses, the building in this picture has been built up over hundreds of years. Some parts of the south-east wing go back to the 14th century, yet the other side dates from c1600. The clock over the entrance has been marking the passing of time for about 350 years. Richard Townley re-built the central great hall in 1725. The family crest, a sparrow hawk, can be found in many places around the building. The original front of the building dated from c1500, but in 1700 it was removed and used for additions to the north-west wing. Townley Hall really is a gem in the history of Lancashire. Some council-run great houses have an air of poverty about them; but not so Townley. If it was a National Trust property, and the cost was £5 to go in, there would be only a quarter of the visitors. Townley is always busy; all kinds of people visit, including school parties, ladies from the Townswomen's Guild or the W I, and coach parties from all over Lancashire, who are told of the history of Burnley and the Townley family. The two diamonds in the Hall's crown are the chapel and its carved altar piece in a room built entirely of oak. This is the only place in England where you can gaze upon the vestments of an abbot made in c1400, and marvel at the stitching and sewing from 600 years ago.

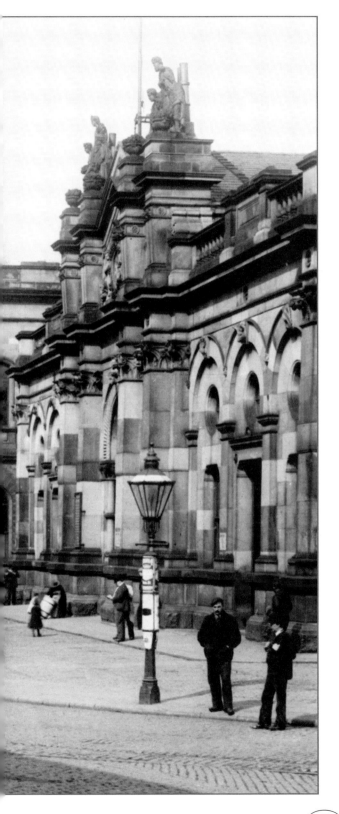

Around Accrington

The name Accrington means 'community where the acorns grow'. It is unusual for a place to take a name from mere acorns, but they were the main source of food for pigs in Norman England, and pigs were an important source of food for many Lancashire villages. The name was written as 'Akarington' in 1194 and 'Acrinton' in 1277. The town grew up on the edge of the Rossendale Forrest. In 1801, Accrington was just a growing village with a population of under 3,000. Before the start of the Great War in 1914, it was an industrial town of over 45,000 people. In 1974, the Municipal Borough of Hyndburn was formed by amalgamating the towns of Accrington, Oswaldtwistle, Church, Rishton, Great Harwood and Clayton-le-Moors.

Accrington, Blackburn Road 1897 40116
Blackburn Road is at the very heart of the town. The first building on the right is the Market Hall, and next to that, in the centre of our photograph, is the Town Hall.

**Accrington
Market Hall 1897**
40117
Here we see a close-up
view of the Market Hall
with its imposing front
and large statues
mounted over the
entrance. There was a
corn market in
Accrington as far back
as the 16th century.
This Market Hall was
opened on 23 October
1868 by Samuel
Dugdale, Chairman of
the local Board of
Health. It contained 80
permanent stalls and
shops, plus 23 lock-ups
in the basement, served
by lifts, for the use of
the stall-holders. Market
days were Tuesday,
Friday and Saturday.
Early closing day was
Wednesday.

Accrington
Blackburn Road 1899

43496

This photograph was taken from outside the Market Hall looking down Blackburn Road towards its junction with Abbey Street. Boots & David Lewis had led the way by being cash-only shops; by 1899, the trend of negotiating over a reduction in the marked price had almost died out. Here we see a Cash Clothing shop on the left, with its 'ready money bargains' piled high in the windows. 'Drink Altham's 2/4d Tea', proclaims the banner further down the street.

Accrington, The Cottage Hospital 1899 43505

The need for Cottage Hospitals was great a century ago, but with the advent of more advanced equipment and specialised nursing, these cottage hospitals, like the isolation hospitals, closed down. Accrington Victoria Hospital took the place of this building, and later a lot of the services were moved to Burnley General Hospital.

Accrington, Blackburn Road c1945 A19004

The railway line to Huncat and Burnley crosses the road here. There was at one time another line down to Rawtenstall, joining what is now the East Lancashire Preserved Railway. As well as having three railway lines, the town also had three turnpike roads. They were the Whalley to Manchester Road (1790), now Abbey Street; the Blackburn Road (1826-7); and the road to Burnley (1838).

Accrington
Blackburn Road c1955 A19013
It is interesting to compare this photograph with picture No 40116
on pages 70 to 71, which was taken from nearly the same spot,
but 50 years earlier. The street is still cobbled, but the tram lines
have gone. Our 'Cash Clothing' shop is now just an ordinary shop
(next to the Savoy Cafe on the right). It looks like a good solid
Silver Cross pram parked outside the tobacconist's on the left of
our photograph.

▼ **Oswaldtwistle, Stanhill Post Office c1955** 0120003

Stanhill is a small community on one of the B-roads between Oswaldtwistle and Blackburn. It was in this building in 1764 that James Hargreaves lived when he invented the Spinning Jenny. Because of his new invention and the new mechanisation it brought about, many people were forced out of their rural homes to work in the factories, and he was forced out of this house and the area. Apart from the ice cream sign and the newspaper advertising board ('Hollywood stars revolt'), the scene could have been anything up to 50 years earlier. There are a lot of these small villages in this hilly agricultural area.

▼ **Oswaldtwistle, Stanhill Road c1955** 0120004

Our photograph shows how near the hills and open countryside are to the towns around here. Oswaldtwistle Moor, to the south of the town, is a lovely unspoilt area of outstanding beauty. 'The 'twist', or meeting of rivers, where Oswald lives' is how the town gets its name. Recently Oswaldstwistle led the way in a new phenomenon: Moscow Mill, Colliers Street, built in 1824, was transformed into a shopping complex. The retail director is Peter Hargreaves, a direct descendent of James Hargreaves, the inventor. The mill has dozens of different shops and stalls, a Textile Time Tunnel that takes you back three centuries, and Stockley Sweets, were you can watch old-fashioned boiled sweets being produced. They also have the world's largest pear drop on display. It is altogether a modern shopping experience.

▲ **Great Harwood The Roman Catholic Church 1898** 40143

Great Harwood lies to the north of Accrington, and commands a lovely part of the Hyndburn Valley. Dominating the east on a hill next to Great Harwood is the Roman Catholic Church of St Hubert, an unusual dedication. It is a large church, and though not as ancient as its neighbour St Bartholomew's, it has some very fine stained glass windows.

◄ **Clayton-Le-Moors
Feathers Hotel c1965**
C111095
Clayton-le-Moors lies four
and a half miles north-east
of Blackburn, and two miles
north of Accrington. The
name comes from Clayton-
Super-Moras, which means
a stretch of barren land.
Here we see the well known
black and white Feathers Inn
at the centre of the town.

Blackburn and Darwen

Before there was Lancashire, there was Blackburnshire: Blackburn was the centre and name of one of the six 'hundreds' of Lancashire. The river through the city is now the Black Water, but in ancient times it was referred to as a stream or burn. Blackburn means 'on the black stream'. The town guards the entrances to the river valleys we have been looking at in earlier pages - the Ribble, the Hyndeburn and the Hodder - and was the starting point for journeys into these areas and over to Yorkshire. A church was recorded in Blackburn in 596AD, and the cathedral church of St Mary stands on that site today. It is the only cathedral in Lancashire. In the Domesday Book, the town is referred to as 'Blacheburne'. For over a century, Blackburn was known as 'the biggest weaving town in the world'; it boasted over 80,000 looms in 130 mills. It was the arrival of the Leeds/Liverpool canal in 1810 that turned a hand-loom cottage industry into the giant of the Industrial Revolution. Coal was mined in Darwen, and there was an alum mine at Pleasington. Many television serials have recently been filmed in Blackburn and Darwen, including 'Where the Heart Is' and 'Hetty Wainthropp'.

Blackburn, The Market and Town Hall 1894 34307
Here we have a busy and bustling view of Northgate. The Town Hall did not need or get a clock, because the Market Hall had the town's clock on a free-standing tower in front of it. The Market Hall and its tower are on the right of our picture, and the square, solid Town Hall is at the side of it. The Market House, as it was called, opened on 28 January 1848. It opened every day except Sunday, and was famous for stalls selling black puddings and sarsparilla. Unfortunately, the old Market House and Clock Tower were cleared away in the 1960s when the new Market Hall opened.

Blackburn, The Market 1894 34306
Blackburn had two markets, the indoor market and an open air one, held every Wednesday and Saturday, when this photograph was taken. Friday was later added to the open market days. Our photograph shows the open market in New Market Street. Here we see the Market Hall (or House) from the rear, and we can also see the back of the Town Hall; its 20ft-high wall guards a courtyard. It was the Market Square that hosted the Blackburn Fair, which was held by Charter every Easter Monday, and then on 11 and 12 May, and also the Winter Fair every 17 October.

Blackburn, Corporation Park 1895 35729
Blackburn possessed six parks, but Corporation Park was the one laid out on clear Victorian lines. Sixty acres were transformed with terraced walks, as we see here. A magnificent palm house, lake and conservatory were also part of this lovely park. Over 60,000 people turned up to see it opened on 23 October 1857. The making of the park provided work for many of the unemployed cotton workers. Notice that every single person in our photograph, from the youngest to the oldest, is wearing a hat. Top hats, boaters, bowlers, billy cocks and bonnets - they are all here.

**A closer look at the people and fashions
in Blackburn, Corporation Park over a century ago** 35729

Blackburn
Sudell Cross 1895
35726

The shops behind the big lamp in the centre of the road are interesting. Next to the draper's shop on the left is Walmsley's Stationers and Bookshop. The large window proudly proclaims that they have a Bible and Prayer Book Department. The horse-drawn tram heads off towards the Town Hall. The Sudell family can be traced back to the reign of Edward VI. They owned land in Blackburn and out at Oozebooth. The family built a large town house on King Street. They also built a large warehouse, and Sudell Court and Sudell's Yard appeared round it. Henry Sudell, the last of the family to live in Blackburn, enclosed Woodfold Park, and built the Hall there. He also bought the manorial rights at Mellor. For all his money (he was a millionaire by 1815), he was a very fair employer, and averted a troublesome strike in August 1818 by agreeing to a 5% rise in wages. In 1827 he lost thousands in overseas trade, and was forced into bankruptcy. He paid his creditors over 19/- in the pound, but they never forgave him; he moved to Bath to live in retirement.

Blackburn
Salford Bridge 1899
43476

Salford was an area of Blackburn; the name derives from 'salix (willow tree) ford'. This is where the old pack horse trail to Accrington and the east crossed the River Blakewater in a shallow ford. It was always a bottleneck, and fifty years before our photograph one form of entertainment would be to sit on the low parapet of Salford Bridge, clay pipe in hand, and watch the farm carts fight their way over the bridge and on to the market. In 1882, under the Salford Improvement Act the 22ft-wide bridge was made 77ft-wide to eliminate this bottleneck, and the river was culverted for over 250ft. By the time our photograph was taken, the river was covered over for over 1,000ft, and Salford Bridge was technically 420ft-wide. We can see the Bay Horse Hotel on the right of our picture, with just the single word Salford on the road sign above the window. The Royal Commercial Hotel can be seen behind it. The river is still there today, running under Penny Street and Salford.

Blackburn
The Exchange 1899 43478

Here we see the grand facade of the Blackburn Exchange & Reading Room, which opened in April 1865. It was known later as the Cotton Exchange. The building, at least the front, is still there today, and is a cinema. Blackburn had had three local newspapers by the time the Reading Room opened. The 'Blackburn Mail' started in 1793; the 'Blackburn Alfred' newspaper was first published in 1832; and the 'Blackburn Times' was first issued on 2 June 1855. We can just make out the advertisement for Whittle Spring Noted Ales to the right of the main door. The spring at Whittle le Woods was known to have healing properties, and when it was made into beer and stout it was said to be good for arthritis and other ailments.

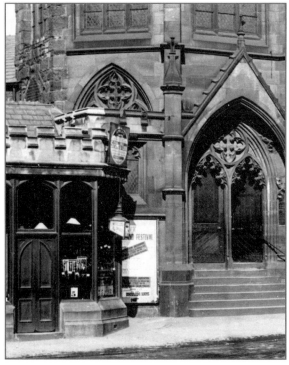

Blackburn, Corporation Park 1923 74052
Here we see the entrance lodge to Corporation Park. No expense was spared in the making of the park and its lodge. The Borough coat of arms and its motto, 'Arte et Labore', is cut into the stone, along with the name of the park over the entrance arch. In the 1950s over 35% of jobs in Blackburn were in engineering, 20% in textiles, and the rest in paper, beer and plastics.

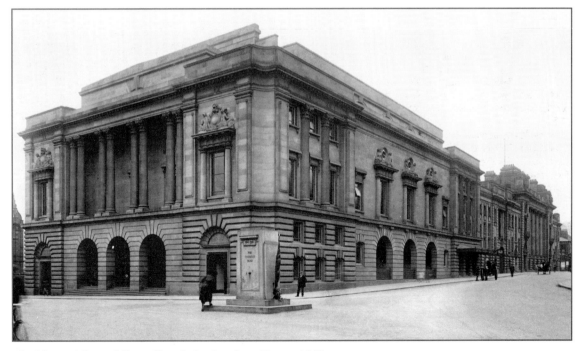

Blackburn, The Public Hall and the Sessions House 1923 74070
Blackburn's Public Hall opened in 1923. The Sessions House is just beyond it on the right. Now called St George's Hall, it is still one of the centres of entertainment in Blackburn.

Blackburn, Queen's Park 1923 74051
Here we see an almost deserted Queen's Park, with just one customer for a rowing boat on the park's lake. The park opened on 20 June 1887 in Queen Victoria's Jubilee year.

Blackburn, The Town Hall c1950 B111003
The town first pushed for a town hall in 1833. The foundation stone was laid on 29 October 1852 by Joseph Fielden, but it was 30 October 1856 before it opened. It has not got the towering Gothic grandeur of some of Lancashire's other town halls, but it does have a certain splendour. It was built at a cost of £29,428 16s 3d. The clock tower and the Market Hall are still here in our photograph, but not for long. Blackburn became a County Borough in 1888. On 5 November 1925 the Blackburn Church Diocese was founded, and the parish church became a Cathedral.

Blackburn
The Boulevard c1960 B111034
This photograph captures the changes that were going on in
Blackburn at the time. There were many Lancashire towns going
through the same revitalisation, but in the frenzy of change many
of the grand Victorian buildings were lost. The buses were mostly
corporation ones, and services were reliable. There was little sign
of the chaos to come on the deregulation of public transport.
Blackburn had started to expand with the canal age. Then, in 1797,
its first turnpike, to Bolton, opened. In 1770 there were 5,000
people living in the town, and by 1811 there were 15,083, three
times that number; by 1835 the population had doubled again. The
railway to Preston opened in 1846, but the station we see here did
not open until 12 September 1886.

Darwen
Whitehall Park 1895 35738
An ornate 19th-century fountain graces the park.
This is one of three parks in Darwen, all very
different. Sunnyhurst Wood is a Nature Reserve;
Sunnyhurst Brook runs through it to join the River
Darwen that gave the town its name. Bold Venture
Park is a disused quarry, with a lake and a
picturesque waterfall. Whitehall Park has always been
noted for its floral displays, and the rhododendrons
make a great show in the late Spring.

Darwen, Whitehall Park 1895 35735

This view from the top of Whitehall Park looks over the flower beds to Darwen beyond. We can make out quite a few of the mill chimneys, but not the most famous of them all, the square 300ft India Mill chimney. Built of local brick with wide stone viewing balconies, it is modelled on the bell-tower of St Marks Square in Venice, and it took fourteen years to build. The River Darwen (a Celtic name) is only 15 miles long before it joins the Ribble near Preston.

Darwen, The Circus c1955 D8010

The Circus, in the town centre, is where five roads meet. It has the usual mixture of banks and public houses on its corners. A National Savings Centre is tucked away on the left of our picture, and the Millstone Hotel is at the far side. Note the very primitive Belisha beacon crossings to guide pedestrians across the large open area.

Darwen
The Market Hall
c1955 D8012
The Town Hall and the Market Hall are on the right. Known as Over Darwen, this was a quarrying and agricultural area before turning to calico printing, weaving and paper making. The Over was dropped 150 years ago. The closed market is open on Monday, Wednesday and Saturday and the open market on Monday, Friday and Saturday. On the skyline you can see Darwen Tower. Built in honour of the Diamond Jubilee of Queen Victoria in 1897, the 85ft tower is 1,300ft above sea level. There is a viewing platform at the top which gives magnificent views over the moors around.

Turton Tower 1897 40106
Turton Tower lies four miles south of Darwen, and four miles north-
east of Bolton. The villages of Turton and Turton Bottoms are next
to the Tower. Turton Tower is basically two buildings, a pele tower
dating from the 1100s, modernised around 1450, and a farm
house or family hall, added in the late 14th century. In 1930 the
hall was sold to the local authorities, and Turton Tower is now open
to the public; it is well worth a visit.

Proud Preston

Preston (which means 'the priest's town') stands on the River Ribble. It is famous for its Guilds, and the Preston Guild Celebrations are held every twenty years. The town is just fifteen miles from open sea, near enough to have docks; Preston has been used as a port since 1360. While Preston does not mark the end of the Ribble, it marks the end of our journey: we have followed the river down from the Pennines, and have seen it pick up all those other rivers on the way - the Calder, the Hodder, the Douglas and many more smaller rivulets that pour into the Ribble. By the time the Ribble reaches Preston it is a deep, mighty river, well able to sustain sea-going vessels.

Preston, The Docks 1893 33097
Before 1892, all ships delivering to Preston would use the riverside for loading and unloading. The year 1892 saw the opening of the Albert Edward Dock Basin: here we see that dock just a year later. The success of the docks can be measured by the large number of ships tied up there. Note how countrified the area behind the quay looks - today, that area is a shopping complex with fast food outlets.

Preston, Old Tram Bridge Over the River Ribble 1893 33100
In 1792, a company was formed by Lancaster merchants; they saw
a canal as a way of getting cheap coal from Wigan and getting
other goods out to the towns in the heart of Lancashire, and to the
growing industrial areas around Kendal in the north. The first
section of the canal, between Preston and Carnforth, opened in
1797. A twelve-mile section from south of the Ribble to near Wigan
opened around 1780. In 1800, with the canal at north Preston, the
company ran out of money. The aqueduct over the River Ribble
was put on hold, and a cheaper alternative, a tramway between the
north and south sections, was built. Here we see the tram bridge,
which was built in 1803. By this time, the southern section of the
canal had been sold to the Leeds & Liverpool Canal Company and
the northern section to the London and North Western Railway
Company. Trams had ceased running over this bridge in 1879.

Preston, Avenham Park and the Park Hotel 1901 33094
The hotel was built by the London and North Western Railway Company for travellers from London to Scotland. At
that time, around 1860, it was considered bad for your health to attempt the whole journey without an overnight stop
half-way, which happened to be at Preston. The Park Hotel cost £46,000 to build; it was designed by Mr A Mitchell.

Preston, The Bridge over the Ribble 1903 50077
This bridge is a railway bridge, and is now part of the west coast main line. Another railway bridge (to Blackburn)
can be seen in the distance. Preston was the centre of a wheel of railway transport: spokes went off to Blackpool,
Lancaster, Blackburn, Manchester, London, Liverpool and Southport. As we can see, the river was used for
pleasure. Boats could be hired from the Pleasure Boat Inn, which is on the left.

Preston, Fishergate 1903 50065
The tower with its clock belongs to the Preston Baptist Church; the Town Hall spire can be seen further up Fishergate. There is an interesting diversity of shops, from a plumber's to the Cocoa Rooms - this has always been Preston's main shopping street.

Preston, The Art Gallery and the Town Hall 1903 50084
The building on the left of our photograph was not just the Art Gallery, but also the Harris Public Library and Museum; it was opened in 1893 as a library, but was not in full use until 1896. The Town Hall, designed by Sir Gilbert Scott, was started in 1862. It burnt down in 1947, and after much debate, the ruins were cleared away in the early 1960s.

Extracts From: Preston, Fishergate 1903 50065
Preston, The Art Gallery and the Town Hall 1903 50084

Hoghton
Hoghton Tower 1895 35719

The home of the de Hoghton family, the house (which is still there today) was mainly built in the reign of Elizabeth I. In the early 14th century, Sir Richard Hoghton and his wife, Sybilla de Lea, presided over an estate which was was already over 40,000 acres. The Tower will always be associated with the visit of James I when he dubbed a simple loin of beef 'Sir Loin'. Thomas Hoghton built most of what we see here in 1565. This was a time of religious troubles, and he left for Belgium in 1569 to spend the last eleven years of his life there. In the Civil War, Sir Gilbert, the Lord of the Manor, was for the King, yet his son and heir Richard fought for the Roundheads. The house was never fortified, so it escaped destruction by Cromwell. Today it is open to the public.

**Bacup
St James Street 1961**
B588050
At this time, local
industry was closing
down; Bacup, which
was off the beaten
track, was looking for
residents to commute
to work in Burnley,
Manchester or other
towns. The town stands
on the young River
Irwell, in the Rossendale
Valley - the name Bacup
means 'in the valley by
the bridge'. Bacup is the
home of the famous
Britannia Coconut
Dancers. The whole
area was also famous
for the manufacture of
slippers.

Chorley, Heading South

Chorley, Market Street c1965 C537055
This is Chorley's main street, the A6, Lancashire's main north to south road; it used to get very busy in the summer. Our photograph was taken before the M6 or the Chorley by-pass opened - Chorley was troubled by heavy traffic for many years. Bleasdale's furniture shop and Yates's Wine Lodge are on the left, and Mangnells and E R Booth are on the right.

Chorley
Market Street c1960 C537016
This photograph was taken further up the street from No C537055.
The shops on the left bring back many memories, and F W Woolworth
is there as well. Chorley Town Hall, with its clock and spire, show up
(right) at the north end of the street. Chorley gets its name from the
smallish but charming River Chor, which runs north of the market town.

Extract From: Chorley, Market Street c1965 C537055
& Chorley, Market Street c1960 C537016

Chorley, Chapel Street c1965 C537018
Chapel Street is framed by the arched entrance to St Mary's Roman Catholic Church and its grounds. The arch is a memorial to a past priest, Father Crank, and was put up in 1913. Even in the 1960s, this part of Chorley was a one-way system to help ease the traffic problems. Today this area is pedestrianised, and the whole of Chorley centre seems to be a one-way system.

Chorley, Astley Hall c1960 C537037
The hall, parts of which date from 1550, has been re-built and added to over the years. It was only two stories high when it was first built - the long gallery and the balustraded top were added in 1685. The Hall belonged to the Charnock, the Brooke and the Parker families before Reginald Tatton gave it to the town as part of a memorial to the local men who gave their lives in the First World War. It was formally handed over in February 1922, and it opened as a museum on 31 May 1924. The Council look after it well, and there is much to see in this fine old building.

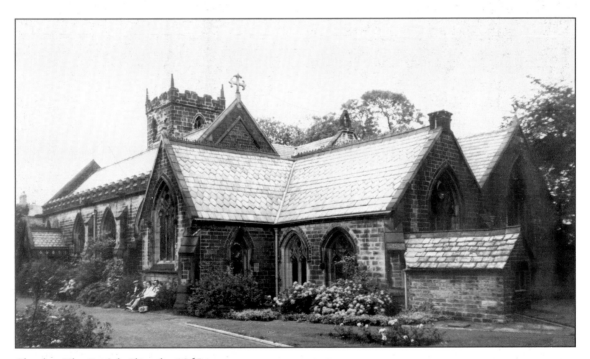

Chorley, The Parish Church c1965 C537057
Chorley's oldest building is the parish church of St Lawrence, which was built in the 14th century. The centre aisle is the original church; the two side aisles were added in c1860.

Adlington
Market Street c1960 A338008
A bread delivery van and some local
traffic make Adlington look busy. The
name of the village comes from an
Old English personal name, Aethel,
meaning 'a noble friend'.

Index

Frith Book Co Titles

www.frithbook.co.uk

The Frith Book Company publishes over 100 new titles each year. A selection of those currently available are listed below. For latest catalogue please contact Frith Book Co.

Town Books 96pp, 100 photos. County and Themed Books 128pp, 150 photos (unless specified). All titles hardback laminated case and jacket except those indicated pb (paperback)

Around Aylesbury (pb)	1-85937-227-9	£9.99	Down the Thames	1-85937-121-3	£14.99
Around Bakewell	1-85937-113-2	£12.99	Around Dublin	1-85937-058-6	£12.99
Around Barnstaple	1-85937-084-5	£12.99	Around Dublin (pb)	1-85937-231-7	£9.99
Around Bath	1-85937-097-7	£12.99	East Anglia (pb)	1-85937-265-1	£9.99
Berkshire (pb)	1-85937-191-4	£9.99	East London	1-85937-080-2	£14.99
Around Blackpool	1-85937-049-7	£12.99	East Sussex	1-85937-130-2	£14.99
Around Bognor Regis	1-85937-055-1	£12.99	Around Eastbourne	1-85937-061-6	£12.99
Around Bournemouth	1-85937-067-5	£12.99	Edinburgh (pb)	1-85937-193-0	£8.99
Around Bradford (pb)	1-85937-204-x	£9.99	English Castles	1-85937-078-0	£14.99
Brighton (pb)	1-85937-192-2	£8.99	English Country Houses	1-85937-161-2	£17.99
British Life A Century Ago	1-85937-103-5	£17.99	Around Exeter	1-85937-126-4	£12.99
British Life A Century Ago (pb)	1-85937-213-9	£9.99	Exmoor	1-85937-132-9	£14.99
Buckinghamshire (pb)	1-85937-200-7	£9.99	Around Falmouth	1-85937-066-7	£12.99
Camberley (pb)	1-85937-222-8	£9.99	Folkestone	1-85937-124-8	£9.99
Around Cambridge	1-85937-092-6	£12.99	Gloucestershire	1-85937-102-7	£14.99
Cambridgeshire	1-85937-086-1	£14.99	Around Great Yarmouth	1-85937-085-3	£12.99
Canals and Waterways	1-85937-129-9	£17.99	Greater Manchester (pb)	1-85937-266-x	£9.99
Cardiff (pb)	1-85937-093-4	£9.99	Around Guildford	1-85937-117-5	£12.99
Carmarthenshire	1-85937-216-3	£14.99	Around Harrogate	1-85937-112-4	£12.99
Cheltenham (pb)	1-85937-095-0	£9.99	Hastings & Bexhill (pb)	1-85937-131-0	£9.99
Around Chester	1-85937-090-x	£12.99	Helston (pb)	1-85937-214-7	£9.99
Around Chichester	1-85937-089-6	£12.99	Herefordshire	1-85937-174-4	£14.99
Around Chichester (pb)	1-85937-228-7	£9.99	Around Horsham	1-85937-127-2	£12.99
Churches of Berkshire	1-85937-170-1	£17.99	Humberside	1-85937-215-5	£14.99
Churches of Dorset	1-85937-172-8	£17.99	Around Ipswich	1-85937-133-7	£12.99
Colchester (pb)	1-85937-188-4	£8.99	Ireland (pb)	1-85937-181-7	£9.99
Cornish Coast	1-85937-163-9	£14.99	Isle of Man	1-85937-065-9	£14.99
Cornwall	1-85937-054-3	£14.99	Isle of Wight	1-85937-114-0	£14.99
Cornwall (pb)	1-85937-229-5	£9.99	Kent (pb)	1-85937-189-2	£9.99
Cotswolds (pb)	1-85937-230-9	£9.99	Kent Living Memories	1-85937-125-6	£14.99
County Durham	1-85937-123-x	£14.99	Lancaster, Morecambe & Heysham (pb)		
Cumbria	1-85937-101-9	£14.99		1-85937-233-3	£9.99
Dartmoor	1-85937-145-0	£14.99	Leeds (pb)	1-85937-202-3	£9.99
Derbyshire (pb)	1-85937-196-5	£9.99	Around Leicester	1-85937-073-x	£12.99
Devon	1-85937-052-7	£14.99	Leicestershire (pb)	1-85937-185-x	£9.99
Dorset	1-85937-075-6	£14.99	Around Lincoln	1-85937-111-6	£12.99
Dorset Coast	1-85937-062-4	£14.99	Lincolnshire	1-85937-135-3	£14.99
Dorset Living Memories	1-85937-210-4	£14.99	London (pb)	1-85937-183-3	£9.99
Down the Severn	1-85937-118-3	£14.99	Ludlow (pb)	1-85937-176-0	£9.99

Available from your local bookshop or from the publisher

Frith Book Co Titles (continued)

Around Maidstone	1-85937-056-x	£12.99	South Devon Coast	1-85937-107-8	£14.99
Manchester (pb)	1-85937-198-1	£9.99	South Devon Living Memories	1-85937-168-x	£14.99
Around Peterborough (pb)	1-85937-219-8	£9.99	Staffordshire (96pp)	1-85937-047-0	£12.99
Piers	1-85937-237-6	£17.99	Stone Circles & Ancient Monuments		
New Forest	1-85937-128-0	£14.99		1-85937-143-4	£17.99
Around Newark	1-85937-105-1	£12.99	Around Stratford upon Avon	1-85937-098-5	£12.99
Around Newquay	1-85937-140-x	£12.99	Suffolk (pb)	1-85937-221-x	£9.99
Norfolk (pb)	1-85937-195-7	£9.99	Surrey (pb)	1-85937-240-6	£9.99
North Devon Coast	1-85937-146-9	£14.99	Sussex (pb)	1-85937-184-1	£9.99
North Yorks	1-85937-236-8	£9.99	Swansea (pb)	1-85937-167-1	£9.99
Around Norwich (pb)	1-85937-194-9	£8.99	Tees Valley & Cleveland	1-85937-211-2	£14.99
Around Nottingham	1-85937-060-8	£12.99	Thanet (pb)	1-85937-116-7	£9.99
Nottinghamshire (pb)	1-85937-187-6	£9.99	Tiverton (pb)	1-85937-178-7	£9.99
Around Oxford	1-85937-096-9	£12.99	Around Torbay	1-85937-063-2	£12.99
Peak District	1-85937-100-0	£14.99	Around Truro	1-85937-147-7	£12.99
Around Penzance	1-85937-069-1	£12.99	Victorian & Edwardian Kent	1-85937-149-3	£14.99
Around Plymouth	1-85937-119-1	£12.99	Victorian & Edwardian Maritime Album		
Norfolk Living Memories	1-85937-217-1	£14.99		1-85937-144-2	£17.99
North Yorks (pb)	1-85937-236-8	£9.99	Victorian and Edwardian Sussex	1-85937-157-4	£14.99
Around Preston (pb)	1-85937-212-0	£9.99	Victorian & Edwardian Yorkshire	1-85937-154-x	£14.99
Around Reading (pb)	1-85937-238-4	£9.99	Victorian Seaside	1-85937-159-0	£17.99
Around Salisbury (pb)	1-85937-239-2	£9.99	Warwickshire (pb)	1-85937-203-1	£9.99
Around St Ives	1-85937-068-3	£12.99	West Midlands	1-85937-109-4	£14.99
Around Scarborough	1-85937-104-3	£12.99	West Sussex	1-85937-148-5	£14.99
Scotland (pb)	1-85937-182-5	£9.99	West Yorkshire (pb)	1-85937-201-5	£9.99
Around Sevenoaks and Tonbridge	1-85937-057-8	£12.99	Weymouth (pb)	1-85937-209-0	£9.99
Around Shrewsbury	1-85937-110-8	£12.99	Wiltshire Living Memories	1-85937-245-7	£14.99
Shropshire	1-85937-083-7	£14.99	Around Winchester	1-85937-139-6	£12.99
Somerset	1-85937-153-1	£14.99	Windmills & Watermills	1-85937-242-2	£17.99
South Hams	1-85937-220-1	£14.99	Worcestershire	1-85937-152-3	£14.99
Around Southampton	1-85937-088-8	£12.99	York (pb)	1-85937-199-x	£9.99
Around Southport	1-85937-106-x	£12.99	Yorkshire Living Memories	1-85937-166-3	£14.99

Frith Book Co titles available 2001

Around Bedford (pb)	1-85937-205-8	£9.99	Lake District (pb)	1-85937-275-9	£9.99
Around Brighton (pb)	1-85937-192-2	£9.99	Liverpool and Merseyside (pb)	1-85937-234-1	£9.99
Buckinghamshire (pb)	1-85937-200-7	£9.99	Around Luton (pb)	1-85937-235-x	£9.99
Cheshire (pb)	1-85937-271-6	£9.99	Northumberland and Tyne & Wear (pb)		
Dorset (pb)	1-85937-269-4	£9.99		1-85937-281-3	£9.99
Devon (pb)	1-85937-297-x	£9.99	Peak District (pb)	1-85937-280-5	£9.99
Down the Thames (pb)	1-85937-278-3	£9.99	Surrey (pb)	1-85937-081-0	£9.99
Heart of Lancashire (pb)	1-85937-197-3	£9.99	Sussex (pb)	1-85937-184-1	£9.99
Hereford (pb)	1-85937-175-2	£9.99			

See Frith books on the internet www.frithbook.co.uk

FRITH PRODUCTS & SERVICES

Francis Frith would doubtless be pleased to know that the pioneering publishing venture he started in 1860 still continues today. A hundred and forty years later, The Francis Frith Collection continues in the same innovative tradition and is now one of the foremost publishers of vintage photographs in the world. Some of the current activities include:

Interior Decoration

Today Frith's photographs can be seen framed and as giant wall murals in thousands of pubs, restaurants, hotels, banks, retail stores and other public buildings throughout the country. In every case they enhance the unique local atmosphere of the places they depict and provide reminders of gentler days in an increasingly busy and frenetic world.

Product Promotions

Frith products are used by many major companies to promote the sales of their own products or to reinforce their own history and heritage. Frith promotions have been used by Hovis bread, Courage beers, Scots Porage Oats, Colman's mustard, Cadbury's foods, Mellow Birds coffee, Dunhill pipe tobacco, Guinness, and Bulmer's Cider.

Genealogy and Family History

As the interest in family history and roots grows world-wide, more and more people are turning to Frith's photographs of Great Britain for images of the towns, villages and streets where their ancestors lived; and, of course, photographs of the churches and chapels where their ancestors were christened, married and buried are an essential part of every genealogy tree and family album.

Frith Products

All Frith photographs are available Framed or just as Mounted Prints and Posters (size 23 x 16 inches). These may be ordered from the address below. From time to time other products - Address Books, Calendars, Table Mats, etc - are available.

The Internet

Already twenty thousand Frith photographs can be viewed and purchased on the internet. By the end of the year 2000 some 60,000 Frith photographs will be available on the internet. The number of sites is constantly expanding, each focussing on different products and services from the Collection.
The main Frith sites are listed below.
www.francisfrith.co.uk
www.frithbook.co.uk

See the complete list of Frith Books at:
www.frithbook.co.uk
This web site is regularly updated with the latest list of publications from the Frith Book Company. If you wish to buy books relating to another part of the country that your local bookshop does not stock, you may purchase on-line.

For further information, trade, or author enquiries please contact us at the address below:
The Francis Frith Collection, Frith's Barn, Teffont, Salisbury, Wiltshire, England SP3 5QP.
Tel: +44 (0)1722 716 376 Fax: +44 (0)1722 716 881 Email: sales@francisfrith.co.uk

---

See Frith books on the internet www.frithbook.co.uk

TO RECEIVE YOUR FREE MOUNTED PRINT

Mounted Print
Overall size 14 x 11 inches

Cut out this Voucher and return it with your remittance for £1.50 to cover postage and handling, to UK addresses. For overseas addresses please include £4.00 post and handling. Choose any photograph included in this book. Your SEPIA print will be A4 in size, and mounted in a cream mount with burgundy rule lines, overall size 14 x 11 inches.

Order additional Mounted Prints at HALF PRICE (only £7.49 each*)

If there are further pictures you would like to order, possibly as gifts for friends and family, purchase them at half price (no additional postage and handling required).

Have your Mounted Prints framed*

For an additional £14.95 per print you can have your chosen Mounted Print framed in an elegant polished wood and gilt moulding, overall size 16 x 13 inches (no additional postage and handling required).

---

* IMPORTANT!
These special prices are only available if ordered using the original voucher on this page (no copies permitted) and at the same time as your free Mounted Print, for delivery to the same address

---

Frith Collectors' Guild

From time to time we publish a magazine of news and stories about Frith photographs and further special offers of Frith products. If you would like 12 months FREE membership, please return this form.

Send completed forms to:
The Francis Frith Collection, Frith's Barn, Teffont, Salisbury, Wiltshire SP3 5QP

Voucher for FREE and Reduced Price Frith Prints

Picture no.	Page number	Qty	Mounted @ £7.49	Framed + £14.95	Total Cost
		1	Free of charge*	£	£
			£7.49	£	£
			£7.49	£	£
			£7.49	£	£
			£7.49	£	£
			£7.49	£	£

Please allow 28 days for delivery	*** Post & handling**	**£1.50**
Book Title	**Total Order Cost**	**£**

Please do not photocopy this voucher. Only the original is valid, so please cut it out and return it to us.

I enclose a cheque / postal order for £ . . . . made payable to 'The Francis Frith Collection' OR please debit my Mastercard / Visa / Switch / Amex card *(credit cards please on all overseas orders)*

Number . . . .

Issue No (Switch only) . . . . .Valid from (Amex/Switch) . . . .

Expires . . . . Signature . . . .

Name Mr/Mrs/Ms . . . .

Address . . . .

. . . .

. . . . Postcode . . . .

Daytime Tel No . . . .   Valid to 31/12/02

The Francis Frith Collectors' Guild

Please enrol me as a member for 12 months free of charge.

Name Mr/Mrs/Ms . . . .

Address . . . .

. . . .

. . . . Postcode . . . .

Free Print - see overleaf